SCARY PLACES
CITIES

Haunted Gotham

by Joyce Markovics

Consultant: Ursula Bielski
Author and Paranormal Researcher
Founder of Chicago Hauntings, Inc.

BEARPORT
PUBLISHING

New York, New York

Credits

Cover and Title Page, © Soare Cecilia/Fotolia, © Andrey Kiselev/Fotolia, © ghoststone/Fotolia, and © Ollyy/Shutterstock; 4–5, Kim Jones; 6, © Sara Krulwich/The New York Times/Redux; 7T, © JannHuizenga/iStock; 7B, Public Domain; 8, © pf/Alamy; 9T, © Merchant's House Museum; 9B, © PHOTOCREO Michal Bednarek/Shutterstock; 10, © Stocksnapper/Shutterstock; 11L, © Marco Cannizzaro/Shutterstock; 11R, © Associated Press; 12, © Hemis/Alamy; 13L, © KieferPix/Shutterstock; 13R, © David Zellaby/CC BY-NC-ND 2.0; 14, © Sean Pavone/Shutterstock; 15, Courtesty of the New York Public Library Digital Collections; 16, © Leonard Zhukovsky/Shutterstock; 17L, © Special Collections and University Archives, Rutgers University Libraries; 17R, © Dmitry Laudin/Shutterstock; 18, © Edmund Vincent Gillon/Museum of the City of New York; 19, © Steve Collender/Shutterstock; 20, © DWlabsInc/iStock; 21T, © Sarony, New York (photographer) - TCS 1.1935, Harvard Theatre Collection, Harvard University; 21B, © kelvinjay/iStock; 22, © Tom Bastin/CC BY 4.0; 23, © Bruno Passigatti/Shutterstock; 24, © Felix Lipov/Shutterstock; 25, Public Domain; 26, © AlbertPego/iStock; 27, © PlusONE/Shutterstock; 31, © Dejawu/Shutterstock and © fotorawin/Shutterstock; 32, © Vitalii Hulai/Shutterstock.

Publisher: Kenn Goin
Senior Editor: Joyce Tavolacci
Creative Director: Spencer Brinker
Design: Dawn Beard Creative
Cover: Kim Jones
Photo Researcher: Thomas Persano

Library of Congress Cataloging-in-Publication Data

Names: Markovics, Joyce L., author.
Title: Haunted Gotham / by Joyce Markovics.
Description: New York : Bearport Publishing Company, Inc., 2017. I Series:
   Scary places I Includes bibliographical references and index.
Identifiers: LCCN 2016038791 (print) I LCCN 2016040772 (ebook) I ISBN
   9781684020201 (library) I ISBN 9781684020720 (ebook)
Subjects: LCSH: Haunted places—New York (State)—New York—Juvenile
   literature.
Classification: LCC BF1472.U6 M343 2017 (print) I LCC BF1472.U6 (ebook) I DDC
   133.109747/1—dc23
LC record available at https://lccn.loc.gov/2016038791

For more information, write to Bearport Publishing Company, Inc., 45 West 21st Street, Suite 3B, New York, New York 10010. Printed in the United States of America.

10 9 8 7 6 5 4 3 2 1

Contents

Haunted Gotham

On the surface, New York City is a shimmering **metropolis**. Taxis and buses whiz along busy streets. Crowds of people fill the sidewalks. Huge buildings jut into the sky. However, among the crowds and skyscrapers are restless spirits **lurking** in the shadows of **Gotham**. They often appear at night . . . reaching out from a cold, dark place. Watch your step, or you might find yourself face-to-face with one of these **urban** ghosts!

In the 11 haunted places in this book, you will explore a **brownstone** doomed by death and an apartment building that's home to the rich, famous, and dearly departed. You'll also visit a **mansion** haunted by a possible murderer, a cemetery where terrible secrets are buried, along with many other terrifying sites.

A Deadly Dwelling

The House of Death, Greenwich Village, Manhattan

The House of Death has earned its horrifying name over many decades. The brownstone, built in 1856, is considered to be one of the most haunted places in Manhattan—and an undeniable den of death.

The House of Death

Soon after the actress Jan Bryant Bartell and her husband moved into the old building in 1957, strange things began to happen. At first, Jan felt an unusual chill in the air. Then more **unnerving** things began to occur.

One day, Jan felt something brush against the back of her neck. When she whipped around to look, nothing was there. She also heard mysterious footsteps and loud crashing sounds. Then there was the odor of something rotten in the air. Most terrifying of all was a "**monstrous moving shadow**" that crept up behind Jan.

After years of spooky encounters, Jan hired a **paranormal** expert to help rid the building of ghosts. Once in the house, the expert felt his body become **possessed** by one of the spirits. The spirit said it would never leave the building! That's when Jan and her husband decided to move out. However, Jan felt that she never truly left the House of Death behind. She was haunted by memories of it until her death in 1974.

The famous writer Samuel Clemens, also known as Mark Twain, lived in the house from 1900 to 1901. Long after he died, one of the building's residents found a visitor in her living room. The shocked woman asked the man what he was doing. He replied, "My name is Clemens . . ." Then he vanished!

Gertrude's Ghost

Old Merchant's House, NoHo, Manhattan

In 1835, Seabury Tredwell, a wealthy merchant, bought a large brick row house in Manhattan. For almost 100 years, the Tredwell family lived—and died—in the house. Some say that at least one family member never left. . . .

Old Merchant's House

In 1840, Gertrude, the youngest of Seabury Tredwell's eight children, was born in the large brick house. According to a family story, when Gertrude became an adult, she fell in love with a doctor. However, her family forbade her to marry him. Gertrude's heart was shattered, and she swore she would never marry. She kept her promise and lived alone in the house for the rest of her life. In 1933, at the age of 93, Gertrude died in her family's home.

Gertrude Tredwell

Less than a year after Gertrude's death, a person working in the house saw "a small elderly woman in a light-colored dress standing in the doorway." Not long after, children playing outside the home were frightened "when the door burst open and a tiny elderly woman flew out onto the high **stoop** in a rage, waving her arms wildly." More recent visitors to the house report bursts of cold air that fill the room where Gertrude took her last breath. A ghostly figure has also been seen gliding up and down the stairs and through the halls. Sometimes, a piano in the home plays on its own!

In 1936, the Tredwells' home became a museum. It's called the Merchant's House Museum and offers tours—including ghost tours!

A Lingering Spirit

The Dakota, Upper West Side, Manhattan

The Dakota is a **lavish** apartment building near Central Park. Built in the 1880s, this famous building is home to the rich and famous . . . and, some say, the dead and buried.

The Dakota

One of the Dakota's most famous residents was the rock-and-roll musician, John Lennon. He moved into the large building with his wife, Yoko Ono, in 1973. From the beginning, there were spooky stirrings in the building. For example, one day John saw a wispy figure of a woman floating in the hallway. Other residents experienced peculiar things as well. There were reports of unexplained footsteps. Also, sometimes, rugs and chairs slid across the floors on their own. However, a truly horrific thing happened in 1980.

On December 8, 1980, John and Yoko were returning to their apartment when a strange man holding a gun appeared. The **crazed** fan squeezed the trigger and shot John in the back four times. John died soon after.

After his death, Yoko saw John sitting at his piano in their apartment. He then turned to her and said, "Don't be afraid. I'm still with you." In 1983, a neighbor reported seeing John near the entrance of the Dakota. He claims that John was "surrounded by an eerie light."

Yoko Ono and John Lennon outside The Dakota

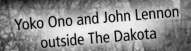

John Lennon was a member of The Beatles, a world-famous band.

The spot in Central Park near where John Lennon's ashes are scattered

An Eerie Inn

The Ear Inn, SoHo, Manhattan

Less than two blocks from the Hudson River is the Ear Inn. The nineteenth-century house has a long history. It's also the favorite hangout of a spooky sailor.

The Ear Inn

Dating from 1817, the brick town house was built as a home for an African-American shop owner named James Brown. In 1833, James sold the house, and it became a pub. Sailors—and, occasionally, pirates who robbed ships on the Hudson River—often went to the pub.

According to **legend**, an old sailor named Mickey was killed in front of the pub. Many believe his spirit still haunts his favorite hangout. People know Mickey is around when the fireplace bursts into flames on its own. Sometimes, people sitting at the bar notice their drinks mysteriously emptying.

In September 2014, a waitress and her friend were napping upstairs at the Ear Inn. The waitress awoke to find her friend staring into space. She asked him what he was doing. He replied, "I'm just saying hello to the strange man standing in the corner." No one was there.

It's believed that James Brown fought in the American Revolution (1775–1783) and worked for George Washington.

"Keep Quiet!"

Morris-Jumel Mansion, Washington Heights, Manhattan

It's little surprise that one of the oldest houses in New York City is home to a restless spirit. The Morris-Jumel Mansion was built by Colonel Roger Morris in 1765. In 1810, a wealthy merchant named Stephen Jumel bought the house for himself and his wife, Eliza. She was very cunning . . . and possibly a murderer.

Morris-Jumel
Mansion

In 1832, Eliza's husband, Stephen, mysteriously fell out of his horse carriage and onto a **pitchfork**. He was seriously wounded, but doctors bandaged him and told Eliza that he would recover. That night, Eliza told the doctors to leave so that she could care for Stephen. The following morning Stephen's lifeless body was found in a pool of his own blood. Had Eliza removed his bandages and let him bleed to death?

Eliza continued to live in the house until her death in 1865. In 1903, the Morris-Jumel Mansion was turned into a museum. Legend has it that Eliza's ghost refuses to leave the house. In 1964, a group of noisy schoolchildren were visiting the mansion when they saw a woman on the balcony. She said, "My husband is very ill. You have to keep quiet." The children told a museum worker about the woman. The worker assured the children that the door to the balcony was locked. When the children toured the house, they noticed a painting of a woman. It was the person they had seen on the balcony. The woman in the painting was Eliza Jumel!

Eliza Jumel

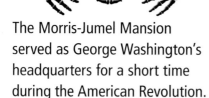

The Morris-Jumel Mansion served as George Washington's headquarters for a short time during the American Revolution.

The Lady of the Lake

Green-Wood Cemetery, Brooklyn

Covering nearly 500 rolling acres (202 hectares) in Brooklyn is the Green-Wood Cemetery. Dating back to 1838, the cemetery is the final resting place for more than 560,000 people. If you look beyond the cemetery's gentle slopes and beautiful trees, you'll discover haunting mysteries buried deep in the ground.

Green-Wood Cemetery

On September 21, 1933, Mabel Smith Douglass was rowing a boat on Lake Placid in upstate New York when she mysteriously disappeared. A witness recalled seeing a woman that looked like Mabel standing up in a rowboat in the lake. Soon after she went missing, police began searching for Mabel. They looked and looked . . . but never found her body.

In 1963, about 30 years after Mabel's disappearance, divers made a shocking discovery. They found what looked like a **mannequin** on the lake's bottom. Upon closer inspection, they saw that the mannequin was actually a perfectly **preserved** body! When they brought the **corpse** to the surface, its fragile skin fell apart. Police later determined that the body was that of Mabel Smith Douglass.

Mabel's body was buried at Green-Wood Cemetery. Today, many believe her **tortured** spirit walks among the tombstones.

Mabel Smith Douglass worked as a **dean** at Rutgers University in New Jersey.

Murder at the Mansion

Kreischer Mansion, Staten Island

If walls could talk, they would have horrifying stories to tell about the Kreischer Mansion on Staten Island. The large house is **plagued** by bad fortune—and death.

The Kreischer Mansion

In 1885, a wealthy businessman named Balthasar Kreischer built two nearly identical mansions for his two sons, Charles and Edward. Balthasar died just a year after the beautiful homes were built. Not long after, the family business burned to the ground. Devastated, Edward killed himself. A few years later, Charles's house burned down. Edward's house—the Kreischer Mansion—remained standing. It became a terrible reminder of the family's **curse**.

Recently, the Kreischer Mansion's awful past came back to light. In 2005, the mansion's caretaker, Joseph "Joe Black" Young, was hired by the **mob** to kill another mobster. Joseph told the man to meet him at the mansion. When he arrived, Joseph drove a knife into the man's body. Somehow, the mobster survived the attack. Joseph then drowned his bleeding victim in a small pool in the backyard. To get rid of the body, Joseph chopped it into pieces and burned it in the mansion's **furnace**! Since that time, the cursed house has sat empty.

Joseph "Joe Black" Young was eventually caught by police. He received a life sentence for the murder.

The Belasco Theatre Ghost

The Belasco Theatre, Midtown Manhattan

Broadway is home to some of the world's most famous theaters. When the curtain drops at the Belasco Theatre on West 44th Street, that's when a ghostly performance begins.

The Belasco Theatre

The top floor of the Belasco Theatre used to be the home of the theater's founder, David Belasco, who died more than 80 years ago. Sometimes, one of the theater's managers hears something strange coming from the locked top floor. It's the unmistakable sound of footsteps!

David Belasco was born in 1853 and devoted his life to the theater. He wrote and directed plays and launched the careers of many young actors. After he died in 1931, actors recalled seeing a dark figure on the balcony after a performance. Sometimes, the figure would even come up to them and shake their hands.

David Belasco

One night more recently, an **usher** working in the lobby jokingly yelled out, "Good night, Mr. Belasco." Suddenly, all the lobby doors swung open at the same time! Chills went up and down the usher's spine. Soon after, the terrified woman quit her job and **vowed** never to return to the Belasco.

It has been reported that at 4:00 P.M. every day at the Belasco, the caretaker's dog growls at an unseen intruder. People wonder whether the dog can see Mr. Belasco's spirit.

21

A Fatal Blow

Haunted Penthouse, Midtown Manhattan

There's a fancy **penthouse** on 57th Street that overlooks Manhattan. No one would ever guess that the apartment was a bloody crime scene—and that the victims of the crime have never left.

The building on 57th Street that's home to the haunted penthouse

Edna Crawford was a showgirl who married a wealthy man named Albert Champion. Not long into the marriage, Edna fell in love with a Frenchman named Charles Brazelle. In 1927, Albert was found dead in a Paris hotel. Edna claimed Albert had died from a "weak heart." However, many people believe that he was murdered by Charles and Edna. Soon after Albert's death, Edna inherited his fortune. She then bought a fancy penthouse for herself and Charles with the money.

Before long, their relationship turned ugly. Charles became violent, and he and Edna fought constantly. Afraid for her life, Edna hired a bodyguard. One night, Charles became so angry that he **fatally** struck Edna in the head with a telephone. Racing to her aid, the bodyguard grabbed Charles and threw him over the balcony of the penthouse. Charles died from his injuries.

The penthouse sat empty for decades. Then a wealthy man named Carlton Alsop purchased it. Soon after he moved in, he heard the clicking sound of high-heel shoes across the wooden floors. Then Carlton began hearing terrible arguments. The ghostly sounds pushed him over the edge. Carlton admitted himself to a **psychiatric** hospital and never set foot in the penthouse again.

Guests of Carlton Alsop claimed to see and hear terrible things at the penthouse, too.

Ghost Station

Old City Hall Subway Station, Lower Manhattan

There's a secret subway station located under City Hall in New York City. It has shiny brass lights, stained glass windows, and curved tile walls. Opened in 1904, this striking station was once bustling with subway riders. Now it's empty, except for the occasional cry of a tortured spirit.

The Old City Hall Subway Station

When workers were building the subway beneath City Hall in the early 1900s, they began to hear peculiar noises after the sun set. *Aaa-ahh! Aaa-ahh!* echoed through the tunnels, along with moaning sounds. They also heard words being chanted in a language they didn't recognize. However, one of the subway workers, a Native American man, understood the words as belonging to the Leni Lenape people. He told his fellow workers about a nearby battle that took place long ago in which many Leni Lenape Indians died. He was sure the sounds were coming from the people who had lost their lives and never received a proper **burial**. According to the worker, they were trapped in a spirit world.

The City Hall subway station closed in 1945 after city officials decided that updating it would be too costly. The station was then sealed for decades. Then in 2004, it reopened briefly for its 100th anniversary. Today, small groups can tour the station. Some visitors still claim to hear the haunting cries of people long gone.

More than six million people ride the New York City subway every day.

Thousands of Corpses

Washington Square Park, Lower Manhattan

Washington Square Park is a lovely place to take a stroll. There's a large fountain, places to picnic, and a beautiful archway. What visitors don't know, however, is that the park sits on top of a mass grave!

Washington Square Park

In 1797, the City of New York created a public burial ground, or potter's field, in the area that's now Washington Square Park. Poor people, criminals, and victims of deadly diseases were buried there in large graves. Sometimes, the bodies were put in wooden coffins and then placed into a large hole. Most often, however, the corpses were simply dumped in the ground.

In the late 1700s and early 1800s, there was an **outbreak** of yellow fever in the city. It claimed the lives of thousands. Many of those who died were laid to rest in the potter's field. Soon, it was completely filled. In 1827, the mass grave was turned into a **public square** and, later, a park. People quickly forgot about Washington Square's **grim** past.

In 2015, city workers digging in the park made a stunning discovery. They found an underground chamber filled with skeletons and coffins! Some experts believe that as many as 20,000 corpses are still buried beneath the park.

The land that makes up Washington Square Park was used as a cemetery from 1797 to 1826.

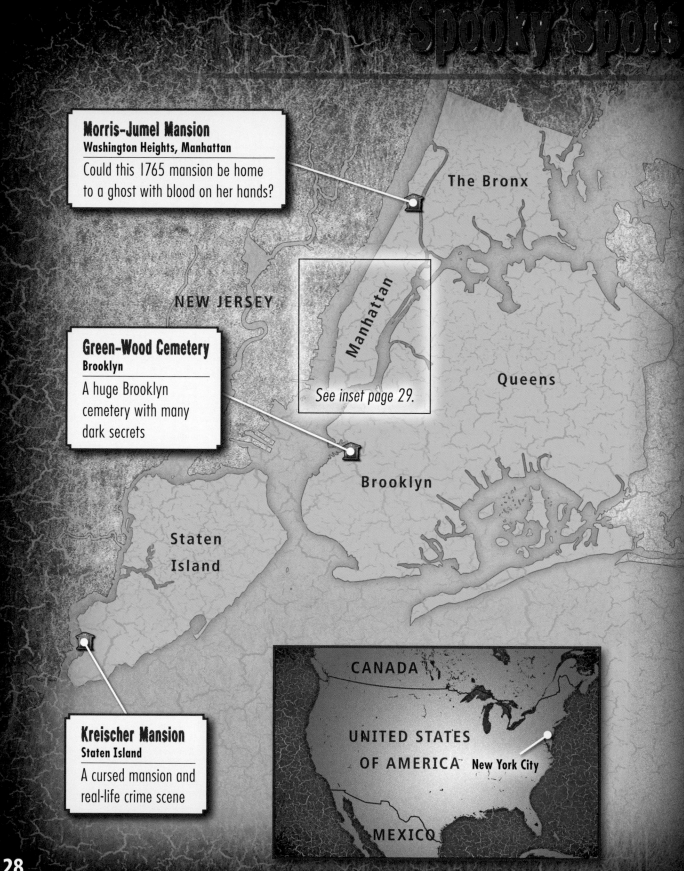

Morris-Jumel Mansion
Washington Heights, Manhattan

Could this 1765 mansion be home to a ghost with blood on her hands?

The Bronx

NEW JERSEY

Manhattan

See inset page 29.

Queens

Green-Wood Cemetery
Brooklyn

A huge Brooklyn cemetery with many dark secrets

Brooklyn

Staten
Island

Kreischer Mansion
Staten Island

A cursed mansion and real-life crime scene

CANADA

UNITED STATES
OF AMERICA   New York City

MEXICO

The Dakota
Upper West Side, Manhattan

Are there more ghosts or famous people living in this luxury building?

Haunted Penthouse
57th Street, Midtown Manhattan

Find out the secrets of this haunted penthouse and its horrific past.

The Belasco Theatre
Midtown Manhattan

Watch out for a ghost that refuses to leave the spotlight.

The House of Death
Greenwich Village, Manhattan

One of the most haunted and terrifying places in New York City

Washington Square Park
Lower Manhattan

Beautiful garden or mass grave? This park has a tale to tell.

Old Merchant's House
NoHo, Manhattan

An old house with a long past—and a devoted ghostly resident

The Ear Inn
SoHo, Manhattan

Beware the spirit of a sneaky sailor at this pub.

Old City Hall Subway Station
Lower Manhattan

Are ghosts lurking in this station forgotten by time?

Central Park

Manhattan

Hudson River

East River

Glossary

brownstone (BROUN-stohn) a house built using a reddish-brown stone

burial (BERR-ee-uhl) the act of placing a dead body in a grave or tomb

corpse (KORPS) a dead body

crazed (KRAYZD) insane

curse (KURSS) something that brings or causes evil or misfortune

dean (DEEN) the head of a college or university

fatally (FEYT-ah-lee) in a manner leading to death

furnace (FUR-*niss*) a metal chamber in which fuel is burned to make heat

Gotham (GOTH-uhm) a nickname for New York City

grim (GRIM) gloomy and unpleasant

lavish (LAV-ish) generous or extravagant

legend (LEJ-uhnd) a story from the past that's not always true

lurking (LURK-ing) secretly hiding

mannequin (MAN-ih-kin) a life-size model of a human being

mansion (MAN-shuhn) a grand house

metropolis (muh-TROP-uh-lis) a large, busy city

mob (MOB) a criminal organization

monstrous (MON-struhss) horrible or frightening

outbreak (OUT-*brayk*) the sudden spread of a disease among a group of people

paranormal (*pa*-ruh-NOR-muhl) events that can't be explained by science

penthouse (PENT-house) an apartment on the roof of a building

pitchfork (PICH-fork) a farm tool with a long handle and sharp metal points

plagued (PLAYGD) bothered by lots of trouble or distress

possessed (*puh*-ZESD) moved by a supernatural power

preserved (pri-ZURVD) kept in good condition

psychiatric (SIKE-ee-ah-trik) relating to mental illness or its treatment

public square (PUHB-lik SKWAIR) an open space in a city or town where people gather

stoop (STOOP) outdoor steps to the front entrance of a house

tortured (TOR-churd) caused extreme pain or suffering

unnerving (uhn-NURV-ing) unsettling

urban (UR-buhn) having to do with cities

usher (USH-uhr) someone who shows people to their seats in a theater

vowed (VOWD) promised oneself something

Bibliography

Gainer, Elise. *Ghosts and Murders of Manhattan (Images of America).* Charleston, SC: Arcadia (2013).

Hladik, L'Aura. *Ghosthunting New York City (America's Haunted Road Trip).* Cincinnati, OH: Clerisy Press (2010).

Revai, Cheri. *Haunted New York City: Ghosts and Strange Phenomena of the Big Apple.* Mechanicsburg, PA: Stackpole Books (2008).

Read More

Hamilton, John. *Haunted Places (The World of Horror).* Edina, MN: ABDO (2007).

Lunis, Natalie. *A Haunted Capital (Scary Places).* New York: Bearport (2015).

Williams, Dinah. *Haunted Hollywood (Scary Places).* New York: Bearport (2015).

Learn More Online

To learn more about haunted Gotham, visit
www.bearportpublishing.com/ScaryPlaces

Index

About the Author

Joyce Markovics lives with her husband in a 160-year-old house near the Hudson River. Chances are that she shares her home with a few otherworldly beings. Her house is very close to spooky Sleepy Hollow, New York, and the historic—and most definitely haunted—Sing Sing prison.